First published in Great Britain in 1997 by
Brockhampton Press,
20 Bloomsbury Street,
London WC1B 3QA.
A member of the Hodder Headline Group.

This series of little gift books was made by Frances Banfield,
Penny Clarke, Clive Collins, Jack Cooper, Nick Diggory,
John Dunne, David Goodman, Paul Gregory, Douglas Hall,
Lucinda Hawksley, Dicky Howett, Dennis Hovell, Helen Johnson,
C. M. Lee, John Maxwell, Patrick McCreeth, Morse Modaberi,
Sonya Newland, Anne Newman, Terry Price, Mike Seabrook,
Nigel Soper, Karen Sullivan, Nick Wells and Matt Weyland.

ISBN 1 86019 556 3

A copy of the CIP data is available from the
British Library upon request.

Produced for Brockhampton Press by Flame Tree Publishing,
a part of The Foundry Creative Media Company Limited,
The Long House, Antrobus Road, Chiswick, London W4 5HY.

Printed and bound in Italy by L.E.G.O. Spa.

The Funny Book of
MOTHERS-IN-LAW

Selected by
Karen Sullivan

Cartoons by

DiCky HOWETT

BROCKHAMPTON PRESS

Bigamy is a crime for which the extreme
penalty is two mothers-in-law.

Old proverb

A woman who was thrown over a banister
by her son-in-law twice within minutes said
last night, 'We never were very close.'

Scottish Express

A mother-in-law is the bark from the family tree.

Anonymous

I can't help detesting my relations. I suppose
it comes from the fact that none of us can stand
other people having the same faults as ourselves.

Oscar Wilde

We had a blessed event at our house —
my mother-in-law finally left.

Old English joke

*"Blimey, Tracie, are you going to
end up looking like your mother . . . ?"*

*"Horace has been quite irritable
since he gave up smoking, Mother . . . ."*

Success is relative.
The more success, the more relatives.

Anonymous

There is but one good mother-in-law
and she is dead.

English proverb

Wife: I am going home to Mother. I should
have listened to her twenty years ago.
Husband: Go ahead, honey. She's still talking.

American joke

I know a mother-in-law who sleeps
with her glasses on — the better to see her
son-in-law suffer in her dreams.

Ernest Coquelin

My mother-in-law has a long-playing tongue.

Anonymous

My mother-in-law has come round to our house at Christmas seven years running. This year we're having a change. We're going to let her in.

Les Dawson

A mother-in-law is what you
inherit when you marry.

English proverb

Many a man would like to drown his troubles, but he can't get his mother-in-law to go swimming.

Anonymous

*"No, we haven't got a dog —
but then you haven't seen my mother-in-law!"*

A homely face and no figure have
aided many women heavenward.

Minna Antrim

Some things go without saying —
like her tongue.

Anonymous

Lady Bracknell: You can hardly imagine that I
and Lord Bracknell would dream of allowing
our only daughter to marry into a cloak-room,
and form an alliance with a parcel.

Oscar Wilde, **The Importance of Being Earnest**

My mother-in-law never wears any lipstick. She
can't keep her mouth still long enough to put it on.

Anonymous

What is the first thing your mother-in-law
does when she gets up in the morning?
She sharpens her tongue.

Anonymous

*"You'll have to accept our marriage
in the end, Mother . . . ."*

Only Adam had no mother-in-law.
That's how we know he lived in paradise.

Anonymous

My mother-in-law always keeps her mirror clean.
Who wants to see dusty wrinkles?

Eddie Berry

A month ago my mother-in-law put mud all
over her face to improve her looks. It improved
them so much she hasn't taken the mud off yet.

Anonymous

1st person: I heard your mother-in-law was
dangerously ill last week.
2nd person: Yes, but this week she
is dangerously well again.

Leopold Fechtner

"Charles has spent years cultivating a cactus
especially for you, Mother."

"You're right, Mother, the label does say,
'kills all known pests'."

My mother-in-law and I never argue.
She always goes her way and I always go hers.

Traditional saying

A woman's place is in the wrong.

James Thurber

He who falls in love with himself
has no mother-in-law.

Traditional saying

Women are natural bitches.

John Carlisle, MP

A mother-in-law should be careful not to
go too far, unless she stays there.

Traditional joke

Certain women should be struck regularly,
like gongs.

Noël Coward, **Private Lives**

She has a tongue that could clip a hedge.

Old gardeners' joke

My mother-in-law is a good eater —
as soon as it's light, she starts to eat.

Henny Youngman

I should, many a good day, have blown my brains
out, but for the recollection that it would have
given pleasure to my mother-in-law; and, even
then, if I could have been certain to haunt her. . . .

Lord Byron, **letter, 28 January 1817**

Surplus: something you have no need for,
like a mother-in-law.

Accountants' joke

*"That reminds me,
when's your mother coming to stay?"*

I hate my mother-in-law. I know
without her I wouldn't have my wife.
And that's another reason I hate her.

Music hall joke

Relations are simply a tedious pack of people, who
haven't got the remotest knowledge of how to live,
nor the smallest instinct about when to die.

Oscar Wilde

1st person: Why are you in such a hurry?
2nd person: I'm on my way to the doctor.
I don't like the look of my mother-in-law.
1st person: Oh, then I'll come too.
I can't stand the sight of mine either.

Anonymous

No men who really think deeply about women retain a high opinion of them; men either despise women or they have never thought seriously about them.

Otto Weininger

There's nothing wrong with my mother-in-law that a good funeral wouldn't cure.

Music hall joke

My mother-in-law has such a pretty chin she added two more.

Eddie Berry

My mother-in-law is so fat, if she was a stripper she'd have to wear a G-rope.

Anonymous

"I think Rupert has had enough pairs of
socks this Christmas, Mother . . . ."

When our relatives are at home, we have to
think of all their good points or it would be
impossible to endure them. But when they
are away, we console ourselves for their
absence by dwelling on their vices.

George Bernard Shaw

One tongue is sufficient for a woman.

John Milton

She talks so much I get hoarse listening to her.

Anonymous

Norman: She's stuck there, all on her own,
day after day, looking after that
old sabre-toothed bat upstairs. . . .
Sarah: Will you not refer to Mother like that.

*Alan Ayckbourn, **Living Together***

My mother-in-law has a slight
impediment in her speech. Every now
and then she has to stop to take a breath.

Anonymous

But there, everything has its drawbacks, as
the man said when his mother-in-law died and
they came to him for the funeral expenses.

Jerome K. Jerome, **Three Men in a Boat**

My mother-in-law has had her face lifted so many
times that now they have to lower her body.

American joke

When they asked me to donate something for the
old-age home, I offered them my mother-in-law.

Mike Seabrook

*'Hang about — if we are the first man and woman,
then who created that mother-in-law over there . . . ?"*

Take a close up of a woman past sixty! You might
as well use a picture of a relief map of Ireland!

Nancy Astor

Is your mother outspoken?
Not by anyone I know of.

Eddie Berry

The awe and dread with which the untutored
savage contemplates his mother-in-law are
amongst the most familiar facts of anthropology.

James Frazer, **The Golden Bough**

I'd like to smother my mother-in-law in diamonds
— but there must be a cheaper way.

Anonymous

*"Stop groaning,
I'm sure Mother didn't mean to sit on you!"*

27

Mixed emotion: watching your mother-in-law
drive off a cliff in your new car.

Anonymous

I'm sorry to hear that your mother-in-law died.
What was the complaint?
I haven't heard any, so far.

Traditional joke

But as to women, who can penetrate
The real sufferings of their condition?
Man's very sympathy with their estate
Has much of selfishness and more suspicion.
Their love, their virtue, beauty, education,
But form good housekeepers, to breed a nation.

Lord Byron

Think you've got troubles?
My mother-in-law has a twin sister.

Jewish joke

*"Well, go on Mother
ask him about his body-building course."*

I don't care if it is a long way, go down and pick Mother up this instant!"

Woman — an angel of truth, a demon of fiction,
Woman's the greatest of all contradictions;
Afraid of a wasp, she'll scream at a mouse,
She'll attack the husband who's big as a house,
She'll take him for better, she'll take him for worse,
She'll break open his head and then be his nurse.
And when he is well and can get out of bed,
She'll take up the saucepan and shy at his head.
Hateful, deceitful, keen-sighted, blind,
Crafty, simple, cruel and kind,
Lifts a man up, casts a man down,
Makes him a king, then makes him a clown;
In the morning she will, in the evening she won't
And you're always expecting she does,
But she don't.

Max Miller

My car has had stereo for a long time — my wife
in the front and my mother-in-law in the back.

Anonymous

I confidently expect that we [civil
servants] shall continue to be grouped
with mothers-in-law and Wigan Pier as
one of the recognised objects of ridicule.

Edward Bridges, **Portrait of a Profession**

When I was your age I had been an inconsolable
widower for three months, and was already paying
my addresses to your admirable mother.

Oscar Wilde, **An Ideal Husband**

My mother-in-law insists she's not fat —
just that she's three feet too short for her body.

Anonymous

My mother-in-law thinks I'm effeminate:
but I don't mind, compared to her I am.

Les Dawson's Joke Book

"At least with all this snow your mother won't be visiting us for a while . . . ."

"That was silly —
inviting Mother to take a stroll around your window box!"

34

A poor relation is the most irrelevant thing in nature, a piece of impertinent correspondence, an odious approximation, a haunting conscience, a preposterous shadow, lengthening in the noon-tide of our prosperity. . . . He is known by his knock.

Charles Lamb

As cold as a mother-in-law's kiss.

Traditional saying

If women were as fastidious as men, morally or physically, there would be an end of the race.

George Bernard Shaw

Be kind to your mother-in-law, baby-sitters are expensive.

Anonymous

I haven't spoken to my mother-in-law for eighteen
months: well, I don't like to interrupt her.

Ken Dodd's Joke Book

Hello! Is that the police station?

Yes.

Have any lunatics escaped near here recently?

Not that I know of, sir.

Oh!

Why do you ask?

Someone's run off with my mother-in-law.

Music hall joke

My mother-in-law is over eighty and still doesn't
need glasses; drinks right out of the bottle.

Henny Youngman

*"Well don't just sit there screaming —
get your mother to scare it away!"*

"Pay no attention Mother. He's just waiting to video
something silly so he can send it to Jeremy Beadle."

A man was driving along happily minding his own
business when all of a sudden his mother-in-law
came tearing around the corner in the opposite
direction on the wrong side of the road. Passing
him, she rolled down the window and shouted 'Pig!'
The man, quite astonished by this insult, went on
his way, muttering, 'Silly old cow.' On turning the
corner he drove straight into a herd of pigs.

Country joke

My mother-in-law said to me: Oh George,
you must come and live in Suffolk.
It's such a wonderful place for widows.

Cynthia Isserlis

My mother-in-law talks so much —
last summer her tongue got sunburned.

Anonymous

The family tree is worth bragging about
if it has consistently produced good
timber, and not just nuts.

Glen Wheeler

Lord, confound this surly sister,
Blight her brow with blotch and blister,
Cramp her larynx, lung and liver,
In her guts a galling give her.

John Millington Synge

Henry: My mother-in-law made me a very
unusual dinner last night: toad in the hole.
John: What's so unusual about that?
Henry: She used real toads.
John: Thank goodness she didn't
try to make spotted dick!

Pub saying

*"It's your mother,
the female impersonator."*

Untidy is perhaps too mild a word; slut would be a better one. Being a slut is of course partly a matter of bad luck as well as bad management: things just do boil over oftener, fuses blow sooner, front doors bang leaving us outside in our dressing-gowns; but it goes deeper than bad luck. We are not actually incapable of cleaning our homes: but we are liable to reorganize instead of scrub; we do our cleaning in a series of periodic assaults. A mother-in-law has only to appear over the horizon and we act like the murderer in a Ray Bradbury story who kept on wiping the finger prints off the fruit at the bottom of the bowl. We work in a frenzy; but the frenzy usually subsides before we have got everything back into the cupboards again.

Katharine Whitehorn

She is the happiest wife that marries
the son of a dead mother.

English proverb

*"It hasn't got a botanical name —
I call it 'mother-in-law's head'."*

"Don't call the police yet,
Mother, the place is in an absolute mess."

I haven't enjoyed meself so much since the mother-in-law got sent off against Wakefield Trinity.

Les Dawson

Mothers-in-law arrive on the twelve o'clock broom.

English proverb

Fred: My mother-in-law converted me to religion.
Frank: Your mother-in-law converted you to religion? How did she do that?
Fred: Because I didn't believe in Hell until she came to live with us.

Bar-room joke

I just got back from a pleasure trip —
I took my mother-in-law to the station.

Anonymous

Family . . . the home of all social evil, a charitable institution for comfortable women, an anchorage for house-fathers, and a hell for children.

J. August Strindberg

Family jokes, though rightly cursed by strangers, are the bond that keeps most families alive.

Stella Benson

Eve Arnold asked her brother in New York if he had seen his mother-in-law. 'The last time I saw her,' he said, 'she was climbing the Empire State Building with King Kong in her mouth.'

Mike Seabrook

Families are nothing other than the idolatry of duty.

Ann Oakley

"He's only jealous because
you've got his plate, Mother."

This man gets a telegram and he says, 'I'm happy today. I'm a daddy. I'm a daddy — after eighteen years I'm a daddy. And before the happy event me wife went to see a fortune-teller. The fortune-teller said to her, "If it's a boy the father will die. If it's a girl the mother will die." I've got a letter here from me mother-in-law on me father's side. I'll read it to you — from me mother-in-law it says:

Your wife has presented you with a bouncing baby boy.   Both doing well.

That'll tell you what the fortune-teller knows. Here am I, strong as a lion, game for anything. She goes on to say:

P.S. Sorry to say the milkman dropped dead this morning.'
Max Miller

No mother-in-law ever remembers
that she was once a daughter-in-law.

English proverb

A man was just crossing a road on a zebra crossing
when a car came hurtling towards him, and
although he tried to jump out of the way, the car
still managed to catch his side, causing him to be
thrown to the ground. A loud cackling noise could
be heard from the car as it sped away.

A policeman who had witnessed the accident rushed
up to Mr Smith and asked: 'Did you see the driver?
Or remember the car's registration number?'

'I didn't need to,' replied Mr Smith. 'It was my
mother-in-law who did it.'

'How do you know?' asked the policeman.

'Simple!' replied Mr Smith. 'I'd recognize that
hideous laugh anywhere.'

Anonymous

Sometimes you can't tell if a man is trying
so hard to be a success to please his
wife or to spite his mother-in-law.

American joke

*"Mother says
the car's going to be all right!"*

Pakistan is the sort of place everyone should
send his mother-in-law, all expenses paid.

Ian Botham

A mother takes some twenty years to mould her
son in her own image; just to see some other
woman make a fool of him in as many minutes.

Anonymous

My mother-in-law broke up my marriage.
My wife came home from work one day
and found me in bed with her.

Lenny Bruce

My mother-in-law's coming is
another mouth to heed.

English proverb

1st person: Why do you call your mother-in-law Camera? Surely that's not her proper name?
2nd person: I call her Camera because she is always snapping at me.

Anonymous

For eleven years Duncan had put up with the fat, interfering old woman. Now he could stand it no longer.
'She's got to go,' he said to his wife. 'I can't stand your mother another minute.'
'My mother!' exclaimed Duncan's wife. 'I thought she was your mother!'

The Huge Joke Book

Behind every successful man stands a surprised mother-in-law.

Hubert Humphrey

"Isn't that kind, Mother — George is playing you his special arrangement of the 1812 Overture . . . ."

We now have a mother-in-law sandwich:
cold shoulder with salty tongue.

Deli counter joke

Eric: But I will say this for her: there was
one time in my life when I think I'd have cut
my throat if it wasn't for my mother-in-law.

Ernie: How do you mean?

Eric: She was using my razor.

The Morecambe and Wise Joke Book

1st person: Yesterday while hunting you
almost shot my mother-in-law.

2nd person: Sorry, here's my gun.
Have a shot at mine.

Traditional shooting joke

"I don't think Mother's very pleased with the birthday present you bought her."

"Why do we always end up looking after your mother's pet vulture when she goes on holiday . . . ?"

They say every woman has her price.
I've got a mother-in-law you can have cheap.

Music hall joke

There are only three basic jokes, but since the
mother-in-law joke is not a joke but a very serious
question, there are only two.

George Ade

Peter remained on friendly terms
with Christ notwithstanding Christ's
having healed his mother-in-law.

Samuel Butler

The clever cannibal toasted his
mother-in-law at the wedding dinner.

Anonymous

Tom: There's one word to describe
my mother-in-law: temperamental.
John: In what way?
Tom: She's fifty per cent temper,
and fifty per cent mental!

Anonymous

As welcome as a mother-in-law on a honeymoon.

English proverb

Give up all hope of peace so long as
your mother-in-law is alive.

Juvenal

There is no good mother-in-law but she that
wears a green gown [i.e., who is under the turf].

English proverb

"Henry, have you been dishing out your home brew to Mother again?"

Mothers-in-law are not so bad after all; in fact,
most of them are fair to meddling.

Mike Seabrook

I must have women — there is nothing
unbends the mind like them.

John Gay

1st person: I call my mother-in-law peach.
2nd person: That's nice. Is it because
she is soft and sweet?
1st person: No, it's because she's got a heart of stone.

Anonymous

Divorce is the best way of getting
rid of a mother-in-law.

American proverb

Acknowledgements:

The Publishers wish to thank everyone who gave permission to reproduce the quotes in this book. Every effort has been made to contact the copyright holders, but in the event that an oversight has occurred, the publishers would be delighted to rectify any omissions in future editions of this book. Children's quotes printed courtesy of Herne Hill School; George Bernard Shaw reprinted courtesy of the Society of Authors on behalf of the Estate of George Bernard Shaw; *Morecambe & Wise Joke Book* reprinted courtesy of the authors' agents; *A Treasury of Humor*, by Eric W. Johnson, published by Ivy Book, Ballantine Books © Eric W. Johnson, 1989; *The Huge Joke Book* edited by Kevin Goldstein-Jackson, Ernest Ford and A. C. H. Newman, Elliott Right Way Books © A. C. H. Newman, Ernest Ford and Elliott Right Way Books; *The Max Miller Blue Book* © 1975 Robson Books and Barry Took, reprinted courtesy of Robson Books; *5000 One and Two Line Jokes*, compiled by Leopold Fechtner © Parker Publishing Company Inc., 1973.